INCREDIBLE STORIES
YOU NEVER READ

The Uncommon Priest

FEROZ FERNANDES

WestBow
PRESS®
A DIVISION OF THOMAS NELSON
& ZONDERVAN

Copyright © 2019 Feroz Fernandes.

All rights reserved. No part of this book may be used or reproduced by any means, graphic, electronic, or mechanical, including photocopying, recording, taping or by any information storage retrieval system without the written permission of the author except in the case of brief quotations embodied in critical articles and reviews.

WestBow Press books may be ordered through booksellers or by contacting:

WestBow Press
A Division of Thomas Nelson & Zondervan
1663 Liberty Drive
Bloomington, IN 47403
www.westbowpress.com
1 (866) 928-1240

Because of the dynamic nature of the Internet, any web addresses or links contained in this book may have changed since publication and may no longer be valid. The views expressed in this work are solely those of the author and do not necessarily reflect the views of the publisher, and the publisher hereby disclaims any responsibility for them.

Any people depicted in stock imagery provided by Getty Images are models, and such images are being used for illustrative purposes only. Certain stock imagery © Getty Images.

ISBN: 978-1-9736-5087-4 (sc)
ISBN: 978-1-9736-5086-7 (hc)
ISBN: 978-1-9736-5088-1 (e)

Library of Congress Control Number: 2019900436

Printed in Canada.

info@ferozfernandes.com
www.ferozfernandes.com

feroz04fernandes@gmail.com

WestBow Press rev. date: 06/12/2019

This book is dedicated to people who appreciate the straightforward sincerity of priests.

May you enjoy the presence of God.

Contents

Preface xiii
Acknowledgments xv
Introduction xvii

Chapter 1   Do You Trust Him? 1
Chapter 2   Those Wearing Blue Jeans Cannot Read in Church. 3
Chapter 3   Holiness Is Like the Flowing Water 5
Chapter 4   Bring a Pen to Church 6
Chapter 5   Unusual Prayer Request 7
Chapter 6   A Priest's Pulpit Threat Fails 9
Chapter 7   Testing a Priest-Professor's Assumptions 11
Chapter 8   Denying God during Easter Service 13
Chapter 9   "How Old Is God?" 15
Chapter 10 A Priest's Dilemma: To Loan Money or Not 17
Chapter 11 A Priest Uncovers a Gas Station Gimmick 19
Chapter 12 Seminarians Find a Way around Picnic Rules 21
Chapter 13 Pastor Chose Legal Safety over Intervention 23
Chapter 14 The Ministry of the Purse 25
Chapter 15 Red Label Bottle Does the Trick 27
Chapter 16 A Priest and Gender Bias 29
Chapter 17 A Priest Forgets to Instruct about Frozen Fish 31
Chapter 18 Sunday Service from the Balcony 33

Chapter 19	Turning Whiskey into Tea	35
Chapter 20	Fishing for Creativity	37
Chapter 21	"High-Five" Absolution	38
Chapter 22	A Priest Explores Learning, Not Grades	39
Chapter 23	Business Administration Is No Good for Priests	41
Chapter 24	New Rule: NO Adjusting the Thermostat	43
Chapter 25	Cross-Bearer's Burden	45
Chapter 26	A Priest Avoids Wristwatches as a Gift	47
Chapter 27	Appreciating an Unprepared Homily	49
Chapter 28	When There Is a Trust Deficit	51
Chapter 29	Washing Sins in a Small Bowl	53
Chapter 30	Strange Kneeling for Confession	54
Chapter 31	Request to Serve a Footlong Sandwich	55
Chapter 32	Using the Same Condom for Twenty-Five Years	57
Chapter 33	Filling the Blanks in the Musical Notations	59
Chapter 34	The Odd Couple: A Seminarian and a Woman	60
Chapter 35	Practice Makes You …	61
Chapter 36	Faking Authorship	63
Chapter 37	A Priest Fails a Confession Exam	65
Chapter 38	Priest Officiates at a Ragging Event	67
Chapter 39	A Priest Sends Out Novices in Pairs	69
Chapter 40	"What Is a Tampon?" the Priest Asked	71
Chapter 41	A Priest Tells a Lie to Discover the Truth	73
Chapter 42	Dogs Rip Out a Priest's Ear	75
Chapter 43	Telling God to Pack Up and Move	76
Chapter 44	A Priest Wants to Buyback His Vehicle	77
Chapter 45	Coffee with Grumpy Old Men	79
Chapter 46	A Priest, a Marriage Course, and Hunting Stories	81
Chapter 47	Driving on the Wrong Side	83
Chapter 48	Two Bottles of Whiskey	84
Chapter 49	No Mass Due to an Unsafe Environment	85
Chapter 50	Visa Expires in Two Days	87
Chapter 51	Mafia Priest	88
Chapter 52	Cop on Sunday	89
Chapter 53	Innocence during the First Confession	91

Chapter 54	Catholics Demand to Replace Christ Crucified	92
Chapter 55	A Woman Wants a Nun to Baptize Her Child	93
Chapter 56	Priests Partying Early Sunday Morning	95
Chapter 57	Priest Fails to Take His Wife while on a Transfer	97
Chapter 58	Priest Avoids Talking about Mary	99
Chapter 59	Professor Forgets the Question during an Exam	100
Chapter 60	A Priest Called "Sin of the Soil"	101
Chapter 61	The Priest Climbs a Tree to Avoid a Dog Bite	103
Chapter 62	The Priest Receives Tequila during the Offertory	104
Chapter 63	Will the Superior Stop the Bishop from Praying?	105
Chapter 64	No National Flag in the Church Sanctuary	107
Chapter 65	A Priest Asked to Teach the Butterfly about God	109
Chapter 66	A Priest Dares to Clear the Pending Bills	111
Chapter 67	A Priest Catches a Thief in the Rectory	113
Chapter 68	The Church and the Speed of Change	115
Chapter 69	Priest Saves a Life with a Snakebite Stone	117
Chapter 70	Priest Fails to Stop Burial in a Backyard	119
Chapter 71	The Nuns Welcome a Con Priest	121

About the Author 123

Preface

Facts appear like fiction in *The Uncommon Priest: Incredible Stories You Never Read*. This book celebrates the wisdom of the Catholic priests in the mundane world. The short stories offer readers a glimpse into the uncanny conflicts and controversies priests find themselves in. The priests in these stories offer candid responses, baffling us into reflecting on holiness while residing in humor. Ordinary folks do challenge the priests to extend the realms of thought and make faith relevant. *The Uncommon Priest* is a blessing, inspiring hard questions. These true incidents will lead you to discover the creative genius of the priest as never before. The events bring about the genuineness of priests, displaying their fidelity to the faith with a mystical involvement in a given context.

Acknowledgments

This book is a product of constant encouragement from my dear friends: priests, nuns, and colleagues. Your prayers and support turned a dream into a reality. May blessings descend on you always and in all ways.

My brother priests shared their stories candidly during priestly gatherings or in frank conversations. I have interacted with almost every priest in these stories. In telling the stories, I wish to bring to life the human side of a priest, which remains hidden to ordinary people. I thank my priest friends for being patient when I started to ask for details. Although your identity will remain unknown to most readers, people who do know you will discover your story. No harm is intended to anyone or any institution mentioned in the book. Priests do face controversial scenarios. I appreciate my brother priests and their unique contribution to the Catholic priesthood and the people of God. Your stories are now part of a bigger circle of readers.

My thanks to Pete Reinwald, my friend from Chicago. Pete worked to improve my style of writing, guiding me with new insights into my prose. I am immensely grateful to those who contributed significantly to the publication journey and wish to remain anonymous. God bless you always and in all ways.

Westbow Press made my dream into a reality. Thanks to Westbow team members who worked efficiently on the manuscript and gave birth to a new book: *The Uncommon Priest*.

A big thanks to my family, well-wishers, and friends. Your prayers and support keep me moving in challenging directions. I admire you for loving me as a priest.

Introduction

People make a priest, even though he must be ordained by a bishop. His companions also define the priest's upbringing, filled with fun incidents. In this book, you will discover the lighter side of what happens within the walls of the seminary, where priests are trained. How can these stories avoid organizational politics? The events capture conflict and controversies. Priests do face trials from their own bishops, superiors, and people. Courageous priests often defy the mores of the institution while still being faithful to their divine calling. Sheer spontaneity defines these stories. You can call it inspiring or crafty, but each priest found a way around an insurmountable obstacle. Sometimes, people put the priest on the spot. His only response is to admire the opponent. The stories you will read were guarded as a secret, till now.

To be a priest is to be uncommon. But to be uncommon among the priests is a rarity. It can redefine priesthood to stay relevant. I hope these stories, like case scenarios, will enlighten priests to lead their pastoral ministry with creativity and holiness. I look forward to you cherishing reading *The Uncommon Priest: Incredible Stories You Never Read*.

1

Do You Trust Him?

Twenty-two-year-old Cliff told his parents that one of his friends was a priest. Visions of "old and boring" no doubt danced in their heads. One day, Father Francis was invited over for tea. The parents finally got to meet him. And they were surprised to see a trendy young priest.

The casual encounter quickly turned serious.

"On a scale of 1 to 10, how much do you trust my son?" the concerned mother asked.

She wanted a serious answer. Father Francis saw that from the look in her eyes. "I trust all my friends," he said.

She wasn't satisfied. "I don't want to know about others," she said. "How much do you trust my son on a scale of 1 to 10, 10 being the highest?"

She waited for an answer.

"In matters of trust, either you trust or you don't," the priest said. "I cannot grade trust on a scale."

The mother turned silent.

Later, Father Francis explained it to Cliff.

"Trusting does not mean accepting all the wrong choices of the other," the priest told him. "It is to provide a space to be oneself, irrespective of eccentric behaviors."

Father Francis provided an opportunity of hope for Cliff to pursue extraordinary aspirations, without judgment.

Cliff, a successful professional now, still pushes the boundaries of acceptable behaviors. When Cliff is feeling low or super cool, he will text his priest friend.

2

Those Wearing Blue Jeans Cannot Read in Church

Father Edward, a new associate pastor, was ready to begin a Sunday service in a suburban American parish. Aurora, a parish volunteer, rushed to tell the priest that the appointed reader—the master of ceremony for the service—was absent.

"My daughter Jane is ready to volunteer," the woman said. "But there is one problem."

"What can be the problem when reading the word of God?" Father Edward asked.

Aurora said Jane was uncomfortable because she had worn blue jeans to church.

Then she pointed to the church's notice board and said, "Father, people wearing blue jeans cannot be readers during the Sunday service."

Time was running short. The service would begin in two minutes.

"What's wrong with the color blue that the pastor had to bar it from podium appearance?" the priest asked. "What about other colors like green, pink, orange? What about men reading during the Sunday services wearing short pants in summer?"

Aurora pointed to the notice board. "You priests should change it," she said.

Jane served as a reader. Blue jeans were as good as anything else.

3

Holiness Is Like the Flowing Water

Alexander, a student priest, joined three classmates in the DePaul University library to complete an assignment for a course on economics and public policy. The classmates adhered to a different faith than the Catholic priest.

"Do you know he is a priest?" Linda said.

"Are you?" another one asked. The group was surprised that Father Alexander looked no different from the other students and occasionally joined them for bar-hopping at night or beer after the evening class.

"Wow. There is a Catholic priest among us," Erika said. "Father, you are holy, and we are not."

"We all are holy," Father Alexander said. "If the water is dirty, it does not lose its nature to be water. Our nature is holiness."

Then the classmates got on to the business of math, which to some students never loses its evil nature.

4

Bring a Pen to Church

One Sunday afternoon, Father Henry invited his friend, a fellow priest, to join him for lunch in the neighborhood of his Chicago parish. The pastor often bumped into his parishioners in the area.

Sure enough, upon entering the restaurant, Father Henry spotted a parishioner dining with his family.

The pastor waved and sat down with his priest friend. They ordered a vegan meal.

"Give me a second," Father Henry said to his friend.

The young Pastor Henry—always friendly and courteous, with a delightful sense of humor—approached the parishioner and his family. The pastor saw the neighborhood restaurant experience as an opportunity to joke with parishioners he hadn't seen attending church on a Sunday.

"Long time no see!" the pastor said. "Welcome to the church. You don't need to buy a ticket to enter but bring a pen and a checkbook along."

The family attended church the next Sunday and invited Father Henry for brunch at the restaurant.

5

Unusual Prayer Request

Father Brian was in Lisbon, Portugal, for a pilgrimage to Our Lady of Fatima. Father Jack, a pastor based in Lisbon, told the pilgrim priest to visit the shrine of Saint Anthony.

"Anthony was born in Lisbon but is known as Saint Anthony of Padua," Father Jack said.

Padua is in Italy.

Father Brian stood in front of the shrine. Before entering the church, he phoned an ardent devotee of Saint Anthony. "I am just about to go into the church where Saint Anthony was born. Do you have any special prayers I can request for you?" Father Brian asked.

"You know it," Ella responded. "Saint Anthony is the patron saint of lost things."

During Mass, the entry to the crypt remained closed for pilgrims. Father Brian had no such restriction. Alone in the vault, he prayed to Saint Anthony.

On his knees, Father Brian did not know what to ask for himself.

Suddenly, he prayed, "If I lose something, don't bother to bring it back. But if I lose my priesthood, my person, please bring it back."

Father Brian treasures this prayer to be one of the defining faith-moments in his priesthood.

6

A Priest's Pulpit Threat Fails

The front rows were empty in the shrine attached to a monastery. People sat comfortably away from the altar, waiting for the Sunday service to begin.

After the entrance hymn, Father Greg invited everyone to sit on the benches closer to the altar.

A few people scurried into the empty front rows. The priest was not pleased, as some remained unmoved.

Some people even stood outside the church to fulfill their Sunday obligation.

"Outstanding Catholics," Father Greg said. "Standing outside the church."

The priest started to lecture those in the back rows. Then he began to yell at those standing outside.

Father Greg said, "If you don't come forward, I will not start the Mass."

Still, some people refused to budge. Father Greg reluctantly began the Mass.

Later, some concerned priests brought up the incident at the priests' meeting.

"Be courteous when you request the people to come forward, to take a seat on the empty benches," Father Roger, the rector of the shrine, said. "But don't threaten people with ultimatums: if you don't come forward, I will not begin the Mass."

"Remember the Gospel. God heard the prayer of the sinner who stood outside the temple," said a voice from the back of the monastery meeting room.

The thought stopped the discussion.

The priest who chaired the meeting had gotten the message. "At least they are coming for Sunday service," Father Roger said.

7

Testing a Priest-Professor's Assumptions

Father Neil, a visiting priest-professor, began to administer a ten-minute viva exam at an institute of theology. The seminarians were expected to be prepared for the exam and assume any question on the topic for the viva.

"Did you prepare enough for the examination?" professor Neil asked the first student.

"No," seminarian Allan replied honestly.

It left the professor stunned. "If you are not prepared for the exam, you can leave the room right now. Why did you come to take the exam in the first place?" Father Neil shouted at Allan.

Allan left the room, without pleading for a second chance. The embarrassed professor knew he hadn't handled the situation well, so he tested the remaining students with caution.

Later that day, Father Neil invited Allan to attempt the viva, like giving a second chance.

Allan declined, saying, "The rule states that those who fail to pass an exam can retake it after fifteen days."

When it came to honesty, Father Neil thought the student passed the test.

The re-exam never happened.

8

Denying God during Easter Service

During an Easter vigil midnight service in a remote parish, Father Mark demanded responses to renew baptismal promises.

"Do you reject Satan and all his promises?" he asked the congregation.

"I do," a few congregants responded.

Father Mark could barely hear the response. He knew people were dozing during the sermon.

"And all his works?" Father Mark insisted, encouraging a louder response.

The reply remained lackluster.

With irritation in his voice, he asked, "And all his empty promises?"

The low-energy responses continued.

The dissatisfied priest pleaded with the congregation to respond more loudly and to stay awake.

"Do you believe in God, the Father Almighty, creator of heaven and earth?" Father Mark asked.

"No, I do not!" a high-pitched voice shouted from the right side of the altar.

The church fell silent; some woke up in shock.

Five seminarians, wearing dazzling white cassocks, were sitting in front of the man who shouted the wrong response.

"Who is that?" the priest asked, shifting his eyes away from the seminarians to the congregation. "The Satan in you is speaking the truth," the priest said.

The seminarians held their laughter, for they knew the culprit: the parish sacristan, the pastor's trusted right-hand man.

Father Mark, stunned to discover the truth, gave a pep talk to the sacristan after the service.

9

"How Old Is God?"

After a Good Friday service near New York City, Father Nelson was walking back to the sacristy. The parish ministered to the Hispanic population.

A young boy stopped the priest.

"*Hablas español?*" the little boy asked.

"*Poco. Poco,*" Father Nelson said.

The boy's mother could not understand English. She was trying to stop the boy from asking questions.

"How old is God?" the boy asked.

"As young as you are," Father Nelson said.

"But God is our Father," the boy responded. "How old is God?" he asked again.

"God is as young as you and old enough to be our Father," the priest said.

"I am seven years old," he said. "God must be 2,017 years old."

Father Nelson told him God is older than that. So, the boy started to count. "A million, billion, trillion years."

"Why do you want to know how old God is?" the priest asked. Father Nelson did not want to say, "God is eternal."

The boy still counted—one trillion to ten trillion. Then he said something unusual. "The end of numbers is eternity," he said.

Eureka! The boy figured out the age of God!

10

A Priest's Dilemma: To Loan Money or Not

Dennis visited his friend Father Jonathan after almost two decades. Dennis and Father Jonathan resided in the same hostel during their school years.

Dennis introduced his girlfriend, Angel, to Father Jonathan. Angel also was Dennis's business partner.

"We run a garments startup. We buy in bulk and sell to the small retailers," Angel said.

"What brings you to this city?" the priest asked.

"We are about to make a big deal for $800 here," Dennis said.

Angel added, "We are falling short $200."

This was in the late 1990s when credit cards were not standard in India.

"If you loan us the money, we shall return it in two days," Angel said.

Father Jonathan gave them the money, and as promised, he got his money back within two days.

"Thank you so much, brother. Because of you, we made a great deal," Dennis said.

After four days, Angel returned to talk to the priest.

"Father, we need your help again," she pleaded. "My boyfriend is waiting with a business client to close another deal. We are falling short $500."

Just like the previous time, Father Jonathan gave her the money.

The priest never heard from his friends again, who left no contact details.

From then on, Father Jonathan decided to be proactive toward those who came to him with money requests. If someone said, "Father, please loan me $300," he would say, "I want to give you money, not as a loan but as a gift. Don't bother to return it. Use it well."

Once and for all, Father Jonathan avoided the hassle of collecting the small amounts of money he loaned to people, who sought financial assistance from him and promised to return the money in a few days.

11

A Priest Uncovers a Gas Station Gimmick

Father Dominic, a senior priest, asked a younger priest for a ride to a wedding reception, where he was to toast the married couple. They stopped for gas, and the elderly priest offered to pay for it.

After the attendant filled the tank, the young priest, Patrick, hurriedly drove away to make it to the reception on time. Father Patrick was at the wedding hall, about nine miles (15 km) away, when he realized that he never received the change owed to him: about thirty dollars.

The developing country had a high level of corruption. A simple mistake could be part of a bigger scam. Father Patrick decided to test it.

After leaving Father Dominic at the reception, Father Patrick returned to the gas station. He explained the situation, but the attendant wouldn't admit that he had failed to give back the change.

"Let's look at the camera footage," Father Patrick suggested.

The attendant agreed.

The footage showed Father Patrick handing over fifty dollars for twenty dollars in gas and not receiving his thirty dollars in change.

The attendant gave in and gave Father Patrick the thirty dollars.

Father Patrick drove back to the reception and handed the money over to the senior priest, who no doubt added a toast to technology.

"At gas stations, people think it is their negligence to fail to collect the change," Father Patrick said. "People who are uneducated, as well as those in a hurry, stand to lose money to such gimmicks."

12

Seminarians Find a Way around Picnic Rules

Father Dan told the seminarians they could consume one glass of beer during their annual picnic on the beach. The seminary authorities assumed the average size of the beer mug to contain a pint of beer.

The seminarians were known to enjoy more than three or four bottles of beer during the annual picnic. Father Dan intended to avoid public outcry about seminarians drinking beer straight from the bottles. As part of the etiquette, the priest suggested drinking beer from a glass.

The smart seminarians met some local families to borrow beer mugs with the capacity of two pints.

During the picnic evaluation meeting, which included the student beer drinkers, faculty members complained that the seminarians did not comply with the beer-drinking rules.

"The beer glass was larger than we assumed," declared Father Dan. "Tampering with the spirit of the rule makes it unethical."

The staff members also decried the use of indecent language in public during the picnic.

"When was it?" Father Dan asked. "Before or after the drinks?"

The students responded in unison, "After the drinks."

Father Dan then settled the debate:

"We cannot hold them fully responsible under the influence of alcohol," he said.

13

Pastor Chose Legal Safety over Intervention

In a city parish, car drivers parked along the street near the church at their own risk.

One day, a woman walked into the parish office, demanding, "I want to see the church roadside camera footage on Friday midnight to Saturday morning."

Elizabeth, the parish secretary, told the woman that she needed to speak with the pastor.

When the pastor arrived, the woman told him that she had parked her car opposite the church after midnight on Friday.

"When I came to my car in the morning, somebody had cut all the tires," the woman said.

The pastor realized that it was a dicey issue. It could be anything: an insurance gimmick, a gang rivalry, or a misdemeanor.

The pastor leaned toward the side of law and safety of the parish.

"Well, if you want to watch the footage, I need a letter from the police," the pastor told the woman. The police could question the pastor for showing the camera footage of a crime scene to an unauthorized person.

Although the women didn't look like a gang type, she never returned with the letter.

14

The Ministry of the Purse

Father Michael invited a priest friend to join a daylong pilgrimage to Holy Hill in southeastern Wisconsin.

Rose, a woman parishioner, was thrilled that she could drive the two priests to the pilgrimage. She happily shared her childhood memories of the holy place.

Rose then mentioned the husband of a friend, saying he "takes care of the ministry of the purse."

Both the priests were curious and asked what she meant by the ministry of the purse.

Rose described her friend's husband, Trevor, as a silent parishioner who rarely volunteered for church ministry.

"What is the ministry of the purse?" Father Michael asked. "I have never heard of it before. Is it something to do with the church money?"

Rose laughed and said, "It is a private joke among us."

Rose explained that when the women volunteered as lectors, ushers, and money collectors, they didn't like to take their purses along with them.

"We decided to keep all the purses together on one bench," the woman continued. "And we instructed Trevor, who rarely says a word, to keep a watch over the purses."

Rose added, "He stoically sits on the bench, guarding the bags."

So, there you have it: the ministry of the purse.

15

Red Label Bottle Does the Trick

Father Stephen ran a remote mission school for the indigenous people in Asia. The government school inspectors were notorious for their demands of money, sumptuous meals, and liquor during their annual visits.

The priest could not offer money. But he usually laid out a five-course lunch and occasionally served a bottle of whiskey or beer.

However, the inspectors expected good, brand-name liquor. They virtually demanded it.

A negative remark from an inspector would cause unnecessary hardship to the donor-funded, low-budget school.

One year, Father Stephen didn't have any whiskey, so he came up with an idea.

He had an empty whiskey bottle of a brand that was famous in its day: Red Label. He purchased some cheap whiskey at a local store and filled the Red Label bottle to the top.

Father Stephen crafted a story and told the inspectors, "A benefactor friend from Europe gave me the bottle."

The inspectors never looked happier, praising imported liquor from the West.

For the next couple of years, Father Stephen repeated the whiskey bottle trick.

16

A Priest and Gender Bias

Father Clive, a newly ordained priest, had an interview to join a nine-month program on the religious formation and pastoral counseling at a prestigious institute in Southeast Asia.

The priest was confident about meeting the eligibility criteria but had one concern: he was two years younger than the required age.

Father Larry, the priest-director, had a PhD in clinical psychology, which he had earned at a distinguished American university.

During the interview, Father Larry noted, "I see you do not have sisters. You have three brothers. This institute has over two-thirds religious nuns attending the program."

The director expressed his concern that Father Clive might have difficulty interacting with nuns.

Father Clive found this irrational and said, "I never had the problem of relating to women as a result of having no female siblings. What's the difference with nuns?"

Father Larry changed the conversation and began talking about the appointment of bishops in Rome. The director aspired to be appointed a bishop. But when Father Larry realized chances of being designated a bishop were unlikely, he started a new religious congregation.

Father Clive joined the nine-month program. A new director took over a couple of months later.

17

A Priest Forgets to Instruct about Frozen Fish

Father Andrew served in a mission parish on the mountain ranges of western India. The church, located eighty miles (130 km) from a fish market, had recently employed a local man to cook basic meals and manage the vegetable garden.

The mission station depended on the charity of people for necessities. Telephones, refrigerators, and televisions were unaffordable luxuries in the late '90s.

But the parish did have an old freezer, donated by a benefactor.

Max, the new cook, had never seen such an electric gadget.

Early one morning, a villager walked over to offer wild-caught fish for the priests.

Father Andrew had a village Mass that evening.

"There is fish in the freezer to cook for evening dinner," the priest told Max.

Father Andrew expected to return to a nice fish dinner. But he retired to sleep disappointed and wondering what happened to the fish.

The next morning, the priest asked about the fish.

"Fish was spoiled," Max said. "I threw it away."

"Was it smelly?" Father Andrew asked, thinking the freezer had stopped working.

"No, it was hard, like a stone," Max responded. "I tried to slice it with the chopper knife, but I could not. Then I threw it into the river."

"Oh," the priest said.

Father Andrew needed to teach the cook how to defrost frozen food.

18

Sunday Service from the Balcony

Sam and his wife, Susan, had moved into a house adjacent to a century-old church, north of Chicago.

The heritage building lacked modern air-conditioning. Proposals to renovate the church never materialized. As the humidity rose, attendance fell during the summer months. Summer holidays for school children also added to the declining church attendance. The church committee members felt that investing in air-conditioning was too costly, given the number of people who attended in the summer.

The couple fancied themselves as good Catholics, and they invited the pastor over for a house blessing.

After the blessing, the wife joked, "Father, can we sit on our balcony and participate in the Sunday service? You know, we can clearly hear your services in our house."

Sam added with a smile, "We often enjoy your homily in comfort with a cup of coffee."

Susan suggested that they could walk across the street to receive Communion. After Communion, they'd hop back across the street and return to their home.

Father Pat, their pastor, nodded and seemed impressed.

"I will send the collection tray during the offertory time to your house," Father Pat said.

He wasn't finished.

"If there is a second collection after Communion," Father Pat said, "You can drop the envelope in the collection box."

Unlike the parochial priest quoting the rubric, the couple was impressed with the young priest's humorous response.

"They must teach humor in the seminary these days," Susan said.

19

Turning Whiskey into Tea

Father Matt treasured his gift from a well-wisher: a bottle of whiskey.

He worked in a remote mission area where alcohol wasn't available. Even if it were available, of course, it was taboo for a priest to buy alcohol from a liquor store.

Father Matt carried his prized gift in a signature cloth sling bag, which grabbed the attention of two seminarians who were on a monthlong trip to visit missions.

Troubled by what they saw, the two brewed a sober trick. While Father Matt was away without a bag and bottle, they emptied the whiskey into another bottle and filled the priest's bottle with something steeped in consciousness.

Later, Father Matt offered his prize to his fellow priests.

"I have a bottle of whiskey," he announced.

He poured it into the glasses and took a sip, sparking light in his eyes.

"It tastes like tea, man!" Father Matt said in disbelief.

A decade later, the priest was reminded of the incident.

"They fooled me," Father Matt smiled.

And somewhere, two former seminarians, no doubt, continue to roll in laughter.

20

Fishing for Creativity

Father Remi, the head of the congregation, was addressing newly ordained priests. He used a local television commercial to grab attention during the sermon.

"A bird was waiting by the riverside to catch a fish," he began, describing a commercial he had seen. "As the wait was turning futile, the smart bird picked up a piece of white thermocol and dropped it in the water.

"When the fish came to bite the white bait," Father Remi continued with a smile, "The bird grabbed its prey."

Then he delivered the punchline: "Do whatever it takes to proclaim the Gospel."

After the sermon, Father Walter, who was present for the event, said to his fellow priests, "Sometimes the homily starter can damage the message."

Another priest added, "The superior is inviting the 'freshly minted' priests to be creative priests, even if it means to fake a bait."

Bismarck, a journalist, overheard the conversation and couldn't resist commenting.

"Priest as the con artist," he chimed in. "Perfect headline."

21

"High-Five" Absolution

The children were prepared for their first Confession but anxious about the strange experience. They had written their sins on slips of paper.

"Are you Nick?" one boy asked the priest. Father Nick was surprised by the unexpected greeting.

The priest did not insist on being greeted as "Father" Nick. He wanted the boy to have a wonderful experience of the sacrament.

"Yes, I am," Father Nick said. "What can I do for you?"

"I want to confess my sins," the boy said.

Father Nick nodded, admiring the straightforwardness of the child.

The boy knelt before the priest and read the list of his sins from a crumpled piece of paper. Father Nick lifted his right hand to offer a blessing.

As the priest started to say aloud the absolution prayer, the boy jumped up, tapped the priest's hand for a high five, and left the scene with pure innocence.

22

A Priest Explores Learning, Not Grades

Father Robert, a newly appointed director of the prominent Institute for Counselling, stressed strict discipline during the yearlong program. Priests and nuns learned skills for pastoral ministry at this institute. The participants joined the program with high expectations due to the institute's reputation and recommendations from bishops and religious superiors.

Father Robert, the priest-director, demanded that the students spend weekends reading and completing projects. He prohibited participants from going out and visiting friends and family on weekends. But Father Craig, part of a group of thirty participants, explored the city on the weekends.

Someone complained to the director about Father Craig's absence on weekends.

"I don't want to listen to excuses for not submitting projects on time," the director told Father Craig in a personal chat. "I hear you are always away on weekends."

Father Craig had always submitted his project work on time. But Father Robert thought Father Craig was setting a bad example.

"I do not intend to be best in the class," Father Craig told the director. "Nor will I fail, even if I don't study."

Being free from expectations allowed Father Craig to explore new fields of learning. One professor discouraged him from submitting an assignment on dream analysis, as it would exceed the two-page limit for the project. Father Craig did it anyway, maintaining the page limit while adding seven pages of reference material.

Father Craig earned all As except for the director's class, where he got a B+.

23

Business Administration Is No Good for Priests

Father Leo, appointed as an assistant to the director to train seminarians, sought to apply for an online MBA in human resources.

Father Leo dealt with young men preparing to commit their lives to God in service to the people.

Father Leo needed permission from the superior to apply for the MBA program. He put forth the reasons for the field of study: learning skills to ensure high performance and create an atmosphere of motivation among the seminarians training to be missionary priests.

The application was declined.

Father Jacob, the superior, responded, "A master's in business administration is for business people and has nothing to do with priestly formation."

Father Benjamin, a close aide to the superior, suggested to Father Leo, "I think you can get approval to study for a master's in history."

"How is history connected to my work?" Father Leo asked. "I need skill training in personnel management."

History happened to be the personal favorite of Father Leo. "Even when I turn fifty years old, I will still enjoy studying history," Father Leo added.

Father Leo could not convince the authorities, as they remained threatened by new fields of learning.

24

New Rule: NO Adjusting the Thermostat

Father Jackson, a newly ordained priest, joined senior pastor Tim as an associate. When Father Tim took his annual holidays, Father Jackson stressed the status quo in the rectory: no change in the way things were done.

A visiting priest, Thomas, a doctoral student in moral theology in Rome, joined the parish team for two months to cover the pastor's absence. Father Thomas had done so the previous three years during the summer holidays.

The summer was hot, reading just over ninety degrees Fahrenheit (thirty-two degrees Celsius). Father Thomas adjusted the thermostat inside the rectory to seventy degrees (twenty-one degrees Celsius).

"You cannot change things," Father Jackson said.

Father Thomas listened with patience.

"You are here for two months," Father Jackson added. "In the absence of the pastor, I am in charge in the parish."

Father Thomas responded, "My service to the Catholic church is with the same dedication, whether I serve one day, a few months, or years in a parish, or for that matter, anywhere in the world."

Father Jackson was stunned with the reply of Father Thomas. No other issues came up between the two priests.

But Father Jackson turned petty things into rules, with no rationale. The parishioners could not understand why this young priest was so concerned about small issues.

Father Tim, the experienced pastor, adjusted to the realities of pastoral life. Unfortunately, Father Jackson had to go on stress medication within a year.

25

Cross-Bearer's Burden

One summer, Father Alfredo was waiting to begin the Sunday service in a suburban parish. Usually, the number of churchgoers dropped during the summer. That made it difficult for the pastor to arrange personnel for Mass liturgies, like lectors, Eucharistic ministers, ushers, and altar servers.

Only one altar server showed up. Antonio, a senior parishioner, took charge and said he'd be the cross-bearer. The service had no candle-bearers.

A minute before the Mass, two altar servers appeared, but they had to get ready.

Father Alfredo had to delay the service until the two children dressed up.

Some in the congregation appeared puzzled by the delay. Antonio seemed to struggle to be the cross-bearer.

"My back is aching holding the cross," Antonio said. "I am carrying the cross when no one showed up."

Antonio joked with the priest, "Jesus on the cross is looking at others, not at me."

Father Alfredo responded, "The cross is going to heal you."

"How can it be?" Antonio said.

"Look at the cross," the priest said. "When you're carrying Jesus on the cross, He isn't looking at you. He is looking at others. But He is right there with you," Father Alfredo added, signaling the choir to start the service.

26

A Priest Avoids Wristwatches as a Gift

Ignatius, along with his wife, Sharon, and his mother-in-law took Father Jordon to a factory outlet mall in Houston, Texas. Ignatius, a former seminarian, was Father Jordon's senior during priestly studies.

The family shopped for Christmas gifts, including expensive and stylish wristwatches.

Sharon told the priest that she wanted to buy him a wristwatch since they had noticed that he never wore one.

"People have gifted me wristwatches dozens of times," Father Jordon told her. "I always give them away to friends who need them."

But Sharon kept insisting.

Father Jordon came up with an excuse. He talked about a study that showed people were distracted by the shiny watches worn by priests, bishops, and even popes.

"I am not saying priests should not wear a watch," the priest said. "It is just that I am comfortable without one."

After Sharon left, the priest told Ignatius that there was no such study about priests and watches.

Father Jordon's views have changed. He now wears an Apple watch, a motivational fitness device.

27

Appreciating an Unprepared Homily

Early one morning, Father Chris offered a Mass for elderly nuns in a nearby convent. The convent arranged the once-a-week Mass for sisters who could not attend the service in the parish.

After Mass, the priest would join the nuns for coffee. They enjoyed the sermons, and ninety-year-old Sister Mary always found his brief homily especially insightful.

One morning, Father Chris appeared distracted and practically mumbled the homily. He later tried to avoid coffee time with the nuns.

Sister Mary walked up to Father Chris and looked into his eyes as if waiting for an explanation.

The priest kept silent.

"Father, this green chasuble looks good on you," she said.

Father Chris told the nuns that he had a funeral service in an hour and a wedding in the early afternoon. He had spent the previous evening preparing sermons for both occasions.

"It takes a toll on the priest to console a family and after some hours, rejoice with another family celebrating a wedding," Father Chris said, skipping coffee for the day.

Father Chris still remembers the words of Sister Mary.

"A genuine appreciation of me as a priest," he recalls.

He continues to join the nuns for a coffee after the convent Masses.

28

When There Is a Trust Deficit

Bishop Rufus appointed Father Felix to solve a complicated legal problem in a city-parish. The twenty-six-year-old parish trust was in the name of a priest who had died seven years ago. At least eight successive pastors either failed to regularize it or had ignored the issue.

As per the direction of the bishop, Father Felix had started the process to regularize the issue.

Father Felix, studying the situation, took a firm stand. A few parishioners, upset about the proposed solution, actively blocked the priest's plans.

Out of desperation, these parishioners wrote to the bishop, alleging that Father Felix was ignoring their concerns. Father Felix expected Bishop Rufus to discuss and clarify the issue with him, which would be standard procedure.

On the contrary, Bishop Rufus wrote back to the priest and asked about the allegations in the letter.

Father Felix had made strides to solve it, updating pending signatures to regularize the status of the trust. Father Felix's attempts did not go well with the former pastor, Ryan, who had tried for the last seven years to complete the task but could not achieve it.

The allegation letter "smelled of envy," but Bishop Rufus tried to cover it up and blamed Father Felix for the situation.

One day, the bishop met Father Felix during a deanery meeting.

"I am sad when lay faithful talk ill about my priests," Bishop Rufus told Father Felix in a private conversation.

"I am not only sad but demoralized when lay faithful talk about bishops who are involved in scams and scandals," Father Felix responded without mincing words.

Bishop Rufus knew the priest alluded to recent allegations against him; some of which were even reported by the media.

Father Felix added, "When there is a trust deficit …"

The bishop moved away abruptly before the priest could complete his statement.

"First, the bishop should trust his priests," Father Felix said quite loudly.

29

Washing Sins in a Small Bowl

During a weekday Mass, Father Jim invited a six-year-old boy to serve at the altar. Another boy joined them. Neither boy had previously served.

The boys looked into the congregation for their parents, whose encouraging gestures kept them buoyant.

During the offertory, the priest said softly, "Wash me from my iniquity and cleanse me from my sins."

He held his hands out to wash them in a small bowl.

"What sins do you have, Father?" one boy asked Father Jim while pouring the water over the priest's hands.

Father Jim responded, "I have small sins, as small as this vessel."

The priest took a towel to wipe his hands.

"Does that mean if you have big sins," the boy asked, "You wash your hands in a big bowl?"

30

Strange Kneeling for Confession

A young woman knelt to confess her sins during a penitential service.

"I have not come here for Confession," she told Father Julius.

The priest tried explaining to her the virtue of the Christian practice of Confession.

"No need to lecture me about Confession," the woman said. "I understand it."

Father Julius appreciated her honesty.

"I don't believe in Confession," she continued. "I tell Jesus about my sins directly."

The woman explained why it was better to talk to God, not the priest, about sins.

Father Julius listened. Silence followed.

"Thank you, Father," she said. "I am sorry I wasted your time."

Father Julius asked her why she had come to the church. The woman told him that she knelt in the confessional to please her mother.

"The next person coming to you for Confession is my mother," she added.

31

Request to Serve a Footlong Sandwich

Why would Ambrose, an ex-seminarian, insist on serving a footlong Subway sandwich to a priest?

Father Carvalho had been a novice master of the ex-seminarian in a remote place in an underdeveloped country.

"In Europe, people eat a sandwich before work," said Ambrose, recalling Father Carvalho's words. "It's their basic meal for the day."

Ambrose and the seminarians grappled with their idea of a sandwich: two slices of bread with coconut chutney. The seminarians worked as laborers in rice fields, eating just rice and cereal. They failed to comprehend how people survived with only a small sandwich. They had no idea of a footlong Subway sandwich.

Father Carvalho grumbled that the young chaps desired to eat all the time.

"If we were given sandwiches like Subway," said Ambrose, presently working in the United States, "we would have worked harder just to earn a sandwich every day."

Ambrose was amazed to see the size of a Subway sandwich when he started working in the developed world. After twenty-one years, Father Carvalho visited the States. Ambrose, now working in the States, desired to treat the priest to Subway. Unfortunately, that did not happen.

32

Using the Same Condom for Twenty-Five Years

In the mid-1980s, Father Ralph, a moral theology professor, walked into a classroom carrying a condom. He had a license in moral theology from a reputed Vatican university.

"I have been using this for twenty-five years," the fifty-three-year-old priest said.

The seminarians burst into laughter.

The Catholic church prohibits artificial methods of contraception. Since there were no printed images of artificial contraception methods in the moral theology books, Father Ralph showed the students what some items looked like.

Father Ralph's ultimate objective was that the seminarians understand the sin before they administered penance during Confession.

Educated in Latin and Portuguese, Father Ralph made efforts to express in English the teachings of Catholic doctrine in the seminary.

The seminarians remembered the humor resulting from the professor's English translations. But Father Ralph's stern looks buried the giggles in the classroom.

According to the seminary rumor, the condom was purchased back in the 1960s.

"That's enough," the professor said. "Don't touch it. I have to use it next year." He meticulously packed it for the next class demonstration.

33

Filling the Blanks in the Musical Notations

Father Seth, an acclaimed musician, had to seek approval from a committee to add devotional songs to his music album. Some members of the committee held a position due to their office. Some were non-musicians, wielding enormous power in determining approval for the sacred music.

Father Seth failed to comprehend how Father Adrian, a non-musician priest, could have the power to make decisions about music, but it happened.

One day, Father Adrian objected to a particular song, saying, "You see, there are too many empty spaces on the notation bar. And some places have too many notes. Why don't you add some notes in the blank spaces?"

Father Seth was dumbstruck! He had designed the notations to create the effect.

After three months, Father Seth released a devotional music album, with the courtesy of a non-profit organization which sponsored the production cost.

Without a change in the notations, the music sounded uplifting.

34

The Odd Couple: A Seminarian and a Woman

Father Rex asked seminarian David to accompany a tribal woman to the doctor. David played the role of translator, as the woman did not know English. Father Rex had hired the woman and her husband for farm work. The husband still worked on the farm while the wife went to the medical center.

"She is complaining of nausea and constipation," David told the doctor.

After the doctor examined the woman, he looked at the seminarian and asked, "Brother, what did you do?"

David panicked as the doctor told him that she was pregnant. The doctor had thought the seminarian was the father. While the doctor wrote the prescription, David explained the situation.

"Brother, what did you do?" came to be a joke among the seminarians.

35

Practice Makes You ...

Costa, a retired music professor, hesitated to accept a new student: a priest in his early forties. The professor did not know much about the priest. Father Boney, locally famous as a Marian musical organizer, had composed some devotional songs. After writing the lyrics and recording the tunes on his cellphone, Father Boney would approach musicians to arrange the music and acclaimed singers to record it for the music album.

"I want to learn how to write music," Father Boney told the professor.

While accepting the priest's request, Costa said, "Practice makes you ..."

Father Boney abstained from the temptation to complete the famous saying with the common word: perfect.

Costa repeated the statement, "Practice makes you ..." leaving a sense of anticipation to learn the lesson. The professor wanted to hear the word: perfect.

But Father Boney asked, "Practice makes you ... what?"

The professor repeated the statement.

"I don't get it," Father Boney said. "Practice makes you what?"

Then Costa said, "Not every practice makes you perfect. The 'right' practice does make you perfect."

Father Boney learned a valuable lesson: "Just not any practice but the right one."

36

Faking Authorship

Father Rodney appointed seminarians Lionel and Benson to select an English professor-cum-playwright to compose a musical for the annual seminary performance. When the seminarians failed to find a resource person to do it, Benson came up with a strategy.

"If the rector discovers what we are planning, he will never approve it," Lionel said.

The two seminarians read a dozen English plays on communitarian themes from the college library. They selected a play and converted it into an operetta. The musically inclined seminarians set the words to music and told Father Rodney it had been composed by the professor they were supposed to select.

Father Rodney read the lyrics, listened to the music, and nodded in approval, but then there was a problem.

"I want to meet the professor," Father Rodney said. "We can always request his services in the future."

"Yes, the professor has exceptional skill," Lionel told the seminary annual performance committee members.

Benson added, "We have given him an invitation to the annual performance."

After the function, Lionel told Father Rodney that the professor was unable to attend the event. "He had to go out of the state for a seminar," he said.

The seminarians succeeded in their prank. They knew that Father Rodney would have rejected their work, so they faked the authorship, making it appear as scholarly work. There was no English professor. The seminarians had written the lyrics and added dialogue to make the performance relevant to the times.

The seminarians graduated before the next seminary annual performance.

37

A Priest Fails a Confession Exam

Vincent belonged to an indigenous congregation, which was celebrating its hundredth anniversary. A cardinal from the Vatican had ordained him and his companions during the centenary celebrations, six months before completing their seminary studies. Father Vincent and the other newly ordained priest still had to finish some theology courses and pass the exams.

The anticipated ordination before the final exams became a memorable event in the congregation.

All went as planned. Of course, the ordination gave the priests a different status. The new priests attended the classes and cleared their exams, except Vincent.

Father Alarico, known to annoy students during their Confession exams, gave Vincent thirty-eight points, just two points away from passing the test.

Vincent had to retake the Confession exam. But he was upset and refused to retake it.

"Once the chalice is filled with wine, you are a priest forever," Father Vincent told the professor. "Failing the Confession exam will not take away the validity of my priesthood," he said.

Father Vincent received his first assignment rather quickly. He left joyfully to serve in the missions. Recently, Father Vincent celebrated the silver jubilee of his priestly ordination.

38

Priest Officiates at a Ragging Event

The newly arrived undergraduate seminarians had to commute to the university on bicycles.

"It is mandatory to have a bicycle license in this state," Father Cirilo announced during a ceremony to distribute cycles to the students.

"We are pleased to have Tom, the honorable licensing officer, who is a friend of our institution," the priest said. "He suggested we conduct the test on campus and issue the licenses here."

Glen, a senior seminarian, started instructing the new seminarians about the standard test of riding the cycle in a figure-eight formation without stepping down.

"If you fail the test, you will have to repeat it after a week," Glen said. "Until the test is passed, you won't get your cycle."

Most undergrads completed the test. One even showed his skills in slow-cycling, taking his time to complete the test. The volunteers tried to push him off-balance, which resulted in an argument with the organizers.

"This is organized ragging (razzing)," Harold, another senior seminarian, said to stop the unwarranted discussion.

Father Cirilo, who corroborated with the ragging (razzing), disappeared from sight. Tom, who was made to appear as an official, lamented being part of the gimmick.

39

A Priest Sends Out Novices in Pairs

Father Martin did the unexpected: sent out novices walking in pairs into the nearest villages. The priest took Jesus's action literally. Jesus sent his disciples out in pairs with instructions for the journey: take no bread, no bag, no money.

"Don't eat if they give you food," Father Martin said. "Beg for food items and cook your own meal."

The novices were advised to enter only non-Christian homes, avoiding Christian villages. The novices had to return before sunset to report the experience.

The students set out with uncertainty, with no money and no cellphones. The walking distance to the nearest village was around forty minutes.

"How are you?" novice Ivan asked a village woman near the community well.

"Who told you we are not all right?" the woman retorted.

The two novices had to move on.

Nelson, a forest ranger residing in the village, hosted the two novices. Some Christian families invited others. The novices in the town created suspicion among the non-Christians.

After three months, the priest repeated the exercise. Some students had a plan. Each pair spent one hour to create their fake story and prepare possible answers.

"The stories looked real," one admitted, "but the experience turned out empty."

Father Martin never found out about the false claims.

40

"What Is a Tampon?" the Priest Asked

Father Benedict, an Asian priest, entered an American university for a two-year graduate program.

Alexia, sitting beside the priest, said, "My project is about public policy to remove the sales tax on tampons. The tampon tax is unfair and discriminates against women."

The tampon tax is a sales tax on feminine hygiene products. The problem is, tampons are not considered a necessity, like food and medicine. Some states do not treat tampons and sanitary pads as necessities.

Alexia explained that Viagra and condoms were exempt from sales tax. Similarly, there is no tax on items targeted toward men, like razors and Rogaine.

"A tax on tampons is a tax on women," she concluded.

"What is a tampon?" Father Benedict asked her. She covered her mouth with both hands to hide her surprise and then explained it to the priest.

"He asked me what tampons are," she shared with the other classmates.

The classmates thought Alexia was joking.

"I did not know," Father Benedict said.

41

A Priest Tells a Lie to Discover the Truth

Father Andrew discovered that some undergraduate seminarians were involved in local gambling, but he did not know their names. Gambling was taboo, and it was a scandal that seminarians were involved.

The priest had appealed to the students to confess the wrongdoing. The seminarians knew those guilty would be reprimanded, leading to termination of priestly studies.

So, Father Andrew sent the entire group, the innocent and the gamblers, home.

"I want to talk about this issue with your parents at home," Father Andrew said.

He explained his plan to visit the homes of the seminarians, going from the south to the north.

But Father Andrew changed plans and started from the north to visit the homes of the seminarians.

Father Andrew first visited a seminarian whom he suspected of gambling.

"I have gone to all the students' houses," Father Andrew said. "Everyone says that you were among those who gambled."

There were no cellphones or social media for a quick "fact-check." The seminarian could not confirm the priest's story. Several seminarians "spilled the beans." The trick worked.

42

Dogs Rip Out a Priest's Ear

Father Titus made the announcement that people were to tie up their dogs when he came to bless their homes during Easter time. The pastor threatened to avoid the blessing if the dogs were left loose around the house.

A newsweekly got wind of the church announcement and reported it with a headline: "No House Blessing if the Dogs Are Left Loose."

The diocesan officials were disturbed with the reporting. The editor explained that the newspaper has only reported what was announced during Sunday Mass.

A week later, the spokesperson of the diocese called in to report that dogs had ripped out the ear of a priest while blessing the house.

Father Wilson, a missionary priest who was on his annual vacation, had volunteered to lessen the burden of the local pastor in blessing homes. The woman had assured the priest the dogs meant no harm. The next moment, two dogs attacked Father Wilson and threw him on the floor. The dogs had damaged the priest's ear so severely that doctors were unable to stitch it back.

43

Telling God to Pack Up and Move

A business baron bought a Catholic church for commercial use in the northeastern United States. As per canon law, bishop Xavier had to deconsecrate the church for public use. It's like saying a holy goodbye to God.

"Can you really deconsecrate a worship space?" Father Eric, a visiting missionary, asked the bishop.

As Bishop Xavier pondered how to reply, the priest added, "It is like telling God, 'Now you pack up and move to another place. It is not profitable for us to make you stay here.'"

Bishop Xavier admitted that no one had asked such a question before.

After a month, the bishop wrote an email to the missionary priest, stating that deconsecrating the church was the hardest things he had done as a bishop.

44

A Priest Wants to Buyback His Vehicle

Father Edison, a self-trained dentist, traversed the mission areas offering free dental services to the poor. The priest had worked in America for over two years, and generous benefactors from the United States donated his equipment and supplies.

Father Edison installed the dentisty equipment in his Voyager vehicle. Father Edison drove over five hundred miles (804 km) from one location to the other with a pet dog. If the car broke down, the priest would fix it. There was no call for car service in those areas in the late '80s.

The villagers saw such equipment in a vehicle for the first time.

When the priest retired, the religious order superiors did not permit him further trips to the mission land. Father Edison was disappointed. The mobile dental clinic remained unused for years. He tried to find ways to donate the equipment to a local medical center but failed. So, Father Edison fixed the vehicle for regular use.

Father Edison could neither sell the vehicle nor donate it to anyone else. It was a cherished memory. He even did not allow anybody to drive it.

Technically, the vehicle was the property of the order. But practically, no one dared to touch it without the permission of Father Edison. "If you sell my vehicle, I will burn the other cars in the garage," the priest had threatened.

The other priests in the community knew that it was highly likely Father Edison would do so. Therefore, no action was taken.

Finally, a superior and his advisor approached the priest. They had to choose their words carefully. "If you allow it, we'd like to sell your vehicle," the superior said in a low voice.

Father Edison was in his mid-eighties. He knew he would never be able to drive the vehicle again due to his sickness.

"What is the price you intend to get?" Father Edison asked.

"Maybe we can get around $700," the advisor said. The vehicle was rusted and needed total repair.

"Do me a favor," Father Edison said, "I will give you the money and repurchase it again."

45

Coffee with Grumpy Old Men

Father Peter invited himself for coffee with friends staying on a lakeside campsite in northwestern Canada. Dan and Greg lived in recreational vehicles (RVs) for five months, starting in April.

A welcome sign, "Grumpy Old Men," stood between the two RVs, pointing arrows in either direction. Greg and his wife resided in one RV, while Dan and his two cats were in the other.

Each man competed for the title Grumpy Old Man 2 (neither wanted to be the first Grumpy Old Man). Before Father Peter started to sip the coffee, the debate began. The priest took sides, favoring one at a time. But for almost two decades since the guys started staying at the campsite, the verdict had never arrived.

Both men were hospitable toward strangers. They enjoyed their space and stayed out of trouble, enjoying the canopy of trees over their RVs.

Once, Greg was questioned by police as a witness to an incident around the campsite. One who broke the law expected Greg to defend him.

"I see nothing," Greg told the police. "I hear nothing."

Father Peter asked, "Who is Grumpy Old Man number one?" They just pointed at each other with a smile.

Then Father Peter noticed a poster on the wall which read: "There is a fine of five dollars for whining."

46

A Priest, a Marriage Course, and Hunting Stories

In the 1960s, a Canadian couple John and Ann, in their early twenties, attended a marriage preparation class with a priest. Father Barry, a seventy-year-old priest, loved to share stories of missionary journeys and hunting.

"In those days, I would perform sixteen funerals in a day," Father Barry told them. When someone died in the winter, the people would keep the dead bodies for the priest to arrive in the spring. Father Barry conducted funerals *en masse* in the mission land.

The couple had no idea why the priest spoke about the funerals.

Almost every week, Father Barry hunted a deer to feed his six sled dogs. The dogs sledded the priest to Mass centers during winter and spring.

After a while, Bishop Gregory prohibited the priest from possessing a hunting gun due to his age. One day, Father Barry walked into the couple's house to borrow a firearm for hunting.

John recalled, "The priest talked about marriage preparation for only ten minutes. I learned more about the forest, the behavior of animals, and hunting tricks."

After hearing hunting stories and receiving blessings from the priest, the couple was happily married for over fifty years.

47

Driving on the Wrong Side

Bishop Morgan introduced Father Simon, an African missionary, to some First Nation school children in northwestern Canada.

The children looked at the tall, well-built priest.

"He is an ordained priest, but I can't send him right away to the parish," Bishop Morgan said. "He has to learn how to drive a four-wheeler vehicle first in Canada."

The bishop continued, "Where the priest comes from, the steering wheel is on the wrong side of the car. Also, people in that part of the world drive on the wrong side of the road.

"How will you recognize the priest when he comes here?" Bishop Morgan asked the children.

Bishop Morgan realized that the children did not want to say, the priest is black.

After a quick silence, little Taylor said, "It'll be easy to spot him. He will be driving on the wrong side of the road."

48

Two Bottles of Whiskey

Connor, an immigration officer, stopped Father Louis at an airport in Europe.

Connor said, "You don't have a visa to visit this country." The officer instructed Father Louis to return to his home country on the next flight.

Father Louis had worked in Europe on a religious work visa for three years. The priest thought his visa enabled him to visit other European countries.

Father Louis looked forward to meeting up with friends, taking some time off, and joining on a pilgrimage. The disappointed priest could not even shop at duty-free stores.

In a final bid, Father Louis asked the immigration officer, "Can I buy two bottles of whiskey from the duty-free store?"

The officer granted the request, which brought some delight to the priest.

49

No Mass Due to an Unsafe Environment

Simone, a middle-aged woman, demanded daily Mass in a remote mission church. Father Donald did celebrate daily Mass but not in the church. He would drive to senior homes, five-ten minutes away from the church. Each day of the week, Father Donald celebrated Mass in one of the three senior homes. The other days he was celebrating Mass in the church.

The suggestion for daily mass in the church would add another mass for the day. But Father Donald agreed to do so.

Usually, three or four parishioners showed up for daily Mass.

The lack of regular Mass attendance discouraged Father Donald. Also, Simone did not show up for daily Mass. But could not stop the services without a valid reason.

One day, Father Donald opened the church for people to arrive for a weekday Mass. But no one turned up. The priest started the ceremony all by himself.

The next time, only Simone was in the church for Mass. Father Donald declined to celebrate the Mass.

"Go and bring someone along with you," Father Donald told Simone, who showed up for the Mass.

Father Donald stopped celebrating daily Masses when there was only a single woman attending. The decision created an uproar in the parish. The bishop called on Father Donald to restart the services. The priest declined.

"It's against the safe environment policy," Father Donald claimed. "According to the diocesan policy, a priest should not be alone with a woman in the church setting."

50

Visa Expires in Two Days

Father Kumar, an Indian priest, had worked in Canada on a religious work visa. While visiting his hometown, Father Kumar did not notice that his visa was about to expire.

Jason, an immigration officer, told Father Kumar, "Your religious work visa expires in two days."

The immigration officer hesitated to allow the priest to proceed to Canada.

The absentminded priest was stunned by the information. But he said, "Yes, but I still have two days."

The officer allowed Father Kumar to return to Canada. After arriving, Father Kumar renewed his visa and joined the ministry in the diocese.

51

Mafia Priest

It was five o'clock in the morning and forty-five degrees Fahrenheit (seven degrees Celsius) in Canada. Father Robin, a man with brown skin, was fishing on a dock. The cool breeze blew his long hair in all directions. A "high-end" car was parked in a no-parking zone.

Fabian, a white man, parked his car and got out to fish on the dock. After assessing the scene, Fabian cautiously walked toward the dock area. He took a few steps, looked at the man with long hair, and stopped again.

After a few minutes, Father Robin said, "Hey, you. Come up here."

With great hesitation, Fabian moved toward the end of the dock.

"Who are you?" Fabian asked.

Father Robin asked sharply, "What do you mean, who am I? I am the Catholic priest here."

Fabian found this hard to believe. Father Robin invited him for Sunday service.

"What did you think about me?" Father Robin asked him later.

"You looked like a mafia guy," Fabian said. "Your car is like one used by a drug cartel."

Father Robin caught a new parishioner that summer.

52

Cop on Sunday

One Sunday afternoon, Father Oliver was stopped by a traffic officer. Since Father Oliver always obeyed the speed limit on the road, he wondered why the officer had stopped him. Usually, after three services, the priest was exhausted by Sunday afternoon.

"Your car's registration has expired," the traffic officer told the priest.

Father Oliver was unable to settle into his new parish because the residence needed repairs. So, he stayed in a different location and drove to his two other parishes for Mass on Sundays. Father Oliver celebrated three Masses on Sunday; each parish was forty-five minutes driving distance.

"I am sorry, the renewal notice must be at a different address," Father Oliver said. "I did not have the chance to update it due to the transition to the new parish."

The officer stated that it was the owner's responsibility to renew the registration, even without notice.

Assuming the officer to be a Catholic, Father Oliver asked, "Did you go to Sunday Mass?"

The officer admitted he did not attend a church service.

"I am a priest doing my duty, and you stopped me," Father Oliver said. "You, a Catholic officer, did not attend Sunday Mass, but I can't give you a ticket."

The officer allowed Father Oliver to proceed without a ticket. In a couple of days, the traffic officer stopped by the church rectory to meet the priest for a friendly chat.

53

Innocence during the First Confession

Seven-year-old Nash finished his first Confession and ran excitedly toward his friends in the church.

"It's done," Nash said.

Nash started chatting with his friends, who had already finished their Confessions.

Suddenly, the boy ran back to the priest, interrupting another penitent's Confession.

"Father, I forgot to tell you one sin," Nash said.

The priest had another penitent in the confessional.

"Just a minute," Father Marco told the boy. "I need to give to this girl absolution, and then you can come in for your second Confession."

"You see innocence first-hand as the children make their first Confession," said Father Marco while sharing the incident with the catechism teachers.

54

Catholics Demand to Replace Christ Crucified

Catholic parents in one parish asked Father Theodore to replace the image of Christ crucified with that of a risen Jesus.

"Father, our children are afraid to look at the Jesus crucified," the parishioners told Father Theodore. "It is unpleasant for our children to grow up looking at the blood from the side of Jesus."

Father Theodore, unable to convince the parishioners, advised them to talk to Bishop Myles.

"Only the bishop can give you permission," Father Theodore said.

Bishop Myles offered a solution: "For six months, you can have the risen Jesus on the altar façade," the bishop said, "but the rest of the year, it should be Jesus crucified."

The bishop's decision was based on fear of people leaving the Catholic church to join another denomination. A new priest, who was posted after a year, never changed it back to risen Jesus.

55

A Woman Wants a Nun to Baptize Her Child

Olivia approached a pastor with an unusual baptism request.

"Father, I want a nun to baptize my child in your church," Oliva said. Oliva, at thirty-four-years-old, knew that only a priest does the baptism.

Father Ernest asserted that the ordinary ministers of the sacrament of baptism are a bishop, a priest, or a deacon.

Olivia still wanted her intention fulfilled.

"What's the emergency for a nun to baptize your child?" Father Ernest asked.

Father Ernest knew that in times of emergency, the Catholic church allows anyone to baptize, even a non-Catholic or non-Christian.

"Oh, no, Father! You can be there in the church," Olivia replied. "Sister Sophia is our family friend and is currently the Superior General of a congregation."

The pastor said, "If that's the case, Sister Sophia should know who can baptize a child in ordinary circumstances."

Father Ernest referred the case to the archdiocesan office to avoid any further discussion.

A priest from the curia officiated at the baptismal ceremony since the pastor was on leave.

Did the nun indeed baptize the child? Father Ernest could check the baptismal register to find out.

56

Priests Partying Early Sunday Morning

Early one Sunday morning, Gibson, a Houston policeman, signaled a Mercedes to pull over for speeding.

Oscar, the Mercedes driver, thought the policeman suspected him of driving under the influence of alcohol since he had been partying the whole night at a wedding.

There are strict liquor laws in Texas. The state prohibits sales of liquor on Sundays. On weekdays, packaged alcohol may be sold between 10 a.m. and 9 p.m.

Texas prohibits any open alcohol containers inside cars, even on the passenger's seat or back seat. Luckily, there was no liquor in the vehicle.

"What's the reason for speeding up?" Gibson asked.

"We are driving back from a party," Oscar said. "I am driving two visiting priests to a friend's place."

The policeman started to laugh.

Partying till six o'clock in the morning was OK. But Gibson found it interesting that two priests were sitting in the back seat, dressed in their clerical collars and black suits.

Priests partying till Sunday morning was unimaginable.

Gibson let Oscar go with a warning.

Father Hector and Father Nathan felt relieved for wearing clerical shirts.

57

Priest Fails to Take His Wife while on a Transfer

Caroline, a church employee, accompanied Father Jeffery to the local market in the mission station on the archipelago. The mission was in a non-Christian community. The people could not understand that Father Jeffery and Caroline were not living as man and wife.

To make matters worse, Caroline even lived in the rectory. The church authorities failed to arrange a separate residence for her. The authorities often transferred pastors solely based on the information given by Caroline. Sometimes, Caroline also served as an unofficial liaison between the pastor and the local people.

When Father Jeffery got transferred, Flora, a non-Christian local woman, asked the newly appointed pastor, "Why didn't Father Jeffery take his wife along? Is he coming back to take his wife?"

Father Asher, the new pastor, tried to explain that Catholic priests don't get married and that Caroline, who was referred to as Father Jeffery's wife, was a hired employee of the church.

Since Caroline appeared as the pastor's wife to the local non-Christians, Father Asher suggested a change in Caroline's duties and residence. A month later, Father Asher received a transfer order.

58

Priest Avoids Talking about Mary

Father Garrett started researching Mother Mary for a musical. He planned to propagate Marian relevance to the youth through music, dance, and drama.

"Can you talk about Mary?" Father Garrett asked his priest-professor, Turner, who had the reputation of answering questions without giving a clear response.

Father Turner replied, "Yes, but I focus more on Jesus."

Father Turner, now retired, had taught systematic theology for almost four decades in the seminary.

Father Garrett made another attempt.

"Father, you taught us Mariology," Father Garrett said. "I wonder how you would look at Mary from the perspective of the younger generation."

The professor repeated his statement; he focused on Jesus.

59

Professor Forgets the Question during an Exam

Father Tristan, a priest-professor, asked seminarian Bruce to talk about the paschal mystery during the final exam of priestly training. Bruce built up his presentation, quoting scripture, referring to church documents, and citing practical implications.

The exam panel consisted of three priest-professors, who were each allotted fifteen minutes to examine the priestly candidate.

While the others listened, Father Tristan interrupted Bruce.

"What did I ask you?" Father Tristan said.

Bruce turned nervous and for a moment wondered if he was answering the question correctly.

With caution, the seminarian reiterated the question asked by the professor.

"Go ahead, continue," Father Tristan said. "I just forgot the question."

60

A Priest Called "Sin of the Soil"

Father Bruno, a missionary priest, visited his home parish during his holidays. Father Bruno worked in distant lands, taking four-week holidays once a year. The home parishioners waited to hear Father Bruno's sermons and listen to his experiences among the mission people.

Father Austin, the local pastor, disliked sharing the presiding chair for the Mass with any other visiting priest.

Some people asked the pastor to allow Father Bruno to share a sermon about his mission work.

"Father, he is the son of the soil," a parishioner said. "Allow the missionary priest to talk about missions."

Father Austin refused to do it. He even refused to allow visiting priests of the diocese to give a sermon during the Mass. So, other priests would come and concelebrate with the pastor.

One day, Father Austin made an exception and told the missionary priest to preside over the Mass.

"Sin of the soil," Father Austin commented just before walking towards the altar for Mass.

Although disturbed by the comment, Father Bruno still had to focus on leading the congregation in worship.

61

The Priest Climbs a Tree to Avoid a Dog Bite

Father James would do anything to avoid a dog bite, even climb a tree. Father James came in as the new rector of the seminary. Father James knew that the rectory's pet dog, Sam, would identify him as a stranger and try to bite him.

Unfortunately, Sam remained unleashed one day. Before even shouting for help, Father James found himself up in a tree. The dog waited below. Father James panicked and cried for help.

But that morning, the students were away attending college. Luckily, seminarian Jobit, who was resting in the infirmary, heard the priest and rescued him.

Father James told the seminarian that another time he had to climb on the refectory table to avoid a dog bite.

"Fortunately, the dog left quickly that day," Father James said with embarrassment.

62

The Priest Receives Tequila during the Offertory

Dona's family stood with freshly cooked food during the offertory of the Mass. Steam rose above the food like incense, and the aroma filled the pews. Along with the food stood a well-wrapped bottle of tequila. All eyes were on Father Clifford.

"I feel like stopping the Mass and eating the lunch right now," Father Clifford said. The offertory hymn played on.

Father Clifford acknowledged after Mass, "I cannot be a better pastor without the support of the people. I attract two things: food and hate."

"When I am feeling low, you serve me hot coffee, and when it is cold, you give me a shot of tequila."

The people loved their pastor. Father Clifford was known to settle problematic cases with ease and clarity.

The following Sunday, Dona's husband asked, "How was the tequila, Padre?"

63

Will the Superior Stop the Bishop from Praying?

Father Anthony, the Superior General, told Father Adam not to organize a Marian musical play. The charity event would involve acclaimed musicians, choreographers, and singers.

"I command you to stop," Father Anthony told the priest. "Obedience! You must obey me."

Father Anthony was averse to the Marian musical without reason.

After walking out of the superior's office, Father Adam booked Archbishop Emeritus Graham of the diocese to lead people in prayer at the event.

Father Adam re-entered the superior's office and said, "Archbishop Emeritus Graham will be leading the prayer during the event."

Father Anthony appeared puzzled.

"Should I call Bishop Graham and tell him that Father Anthony is blocking him from coming to pray?" Father Adam asked.

"No, you can't do that," Father Anthony said.

Father Anthony failed to stop Bishop Graham, who attended and prayed at the successful event.

Father Adam staged the musical to the Marian devotees, without any hurdles.

Acclaimed musicians, choreographers, and singers offered their services free of charge for the event.

64

No National Flag in the Church Sanctuary

Rafael clandestinely added the national flag in the church sanctuary during the absence of the pastor. Father Jeremy was upset when he returned, as it was done without his permission.

Rafael saw it as a patriotic act to have the flag in the church. He also emailed parish council members, accusing Father Jeremy of being unpatriotic and warning him of dire consequences if the flag was moved.

The emails temporarily stopped Father Jeremy from shifting the flag to a more appropriate place in the church. Many Catholic churches have a national flag and a Vatican flag around the sanctuary. Father Jeremy engaged himself in studying the issue and discovered that even the diocesan cathedral did not have the national flag at the main altar.

Father Jeremy educated the community and said that there was no mention about displaying the national flag in church documents.

"Although there is no prohibition, the liturgy committees do discourage the display of the flag in the sanctuary of the church,"

Father Jeremy said. He added that there were different ways to show patriotism.

"I am going to donate to other parishes," threatened Rafael, who also happened to be a big benefactor to the parish.

The pastor suggested placing the flag in the vestibule.

"It's dark there," Rafael objected. "No one will see."

"Have you seen it recently?" Father Jeremy said. "The vestibule area looks awesome after a recent renovation."

65

A Priest Asked to Teach the Butterfly about God

The third and fourth graders undertook a school project to see caterpillars turning into butterflies.

The chrysalis or pupas were ordered and brought into the classroom. Each child had a chrysalis to track its progress. The children were excited to witness the lifecycle: egg, larva, pupa, and adult butterflies.

On the day the butterflies were ready to fly away, the children gathered around a nearby church. The children and the teachers stood in a circle, with the box of chrysalis covered with a net. It was time to release the butterflies.

As the butterflies found the strength in their wings, each flew in their own time.

One butterfly sat on the church window.

Milo said, "Father, look, the butterfly wants to know about God."

Father Hartman nodded.

"Father, you can teach the butterfly about God," Milo added innocently.

Father Hartman said to Milo, "What can I teach the butterfly about God that the butterfly does not know already?"

"I don't know," Milo said. "You teach him."

Father Hartman said, "What if the butterfly will teach me about God?"

Milo giggled. It was time for the children to return back to school.

66

A Priest Dares to Clear the Pending Bills

Young pastor Edwin, who was entrusted with building a new church, received a transfer order. He tried to negotiate for additional time at his current parish.

"Give me another six months," Father Edwin said. "I will clear the pending contractor bill of $30,000."

Father Roland, the Superior General, declined and said, "You just leave it. It is the responsibility of the congregation to pay the contractor."

The religious order did not pay, even after reminders. The religious order assumed that it was the responsibility of the bishop to pay the amount. Father Edwin, after understanding the new responsibility, tried to raise funds through a charity event. But Father Roland blocked Father Edwin's efforts.

After six months, Father Edwin met Father Roland. "I have told the contractor we will pay back the money," Father Edwin said. " I want to keep my promise to pay on time."

"If the congregation is unable to pay it, grant me a leave of absence for three years. I will serve in America. When I return, I will hand you over $70,000; you pay the contractor, and the remaining is for you."

The superior rejected Father Edwin's proposal of a leave of absence but paid the contractor the next day.

67

A Priest Catches a Thief in the Rectory

Father Simon discovered that money was missing from his room. Parishioners walked in and out unannounced during the rectory renovations. Father Simon left his room unlocked, with personal monies in an unsecured cupboard.

The people working in the rectory confirmed their honesty, as they wanted to keep their jobs.

"I think the money was taken while we were at Mass," Father Simon told the deacon. Deacon Leon also stayed in the rectory during his diaconate ministry.

Father Simon assumed the suspect would know the whereabouts of the parish personnel.

"We need a trick to catch the person red-handed," Father Simon said.

The parish youth were told that Deacon Leon was away on a retreat. Father Simon instructed Deacon Leon to hide in the bathroom during the weekday Mass to see who came into his room. The first attempt failed. Ruben, the suspected parish youth, walked into the rectory on the following day. Ruben called out for Deacon Leon, who remained still in the hideout.

Then Ruben unlatched the cupboard door and picked up the money. Even before Deacon Leon could come out from his hiding place, Ruben latched the cupboard door back to its normal position and left the room.

Deacon Leon jumped out through the room's window into the alley and noticed Ruben zooming out. Father Simon, who had just finished the Mass, stopped Ruben without alarming the people. Ruben denied doing anything wrong.

The wise priest had written down the serial numbers of the currency notes and then put them in the cupboard. Ruben took the bait. The money was tucked into his underwear. When Father Simon threatened to call his parents, Ruben confessed to the crime.

68

The Church and the Speed of Change

Father Kane, a religious order priest, planned a Gospel music concert for the local youth. The priest gathered famous musicians with unique talent.

"Every day, you play music to earn a living," Father Kane said, "but one day, you can do it for God."

The musicians, irregular churchgoers, agreed to render their services without charge.

"Is the program supported by your Order?" a diocesan priest asked Father Kane.

Contrary to endorsing it, his superiors had tried to crush the event.

The program was under an exclusive banner, not supported by the priest's religious order.

"If I say my Order supports the event, the other religious orders will drop out, and the diocese refuses to cooperate," Father Kane said.

The priest created a nonprofit organization to host the event, with the objective to donate profits to charitable causes.

"We live in a world of big mergers and acquisitions," Father Kane told Father Ted, a priest friend. "In the church setting, we are witnessing a lack of cooperation between different religious orders and the diocese, and between different Orders, on petty issues."

"Where the world moves in seconds, the church moves in decades," Father Ted commented.

69

Priest Saves a Life with a Snakebite Stone

One night in India, a deadly poisonous Russell viper bit Rocco, a nineteen-year-old seminarian. The snake left two marks on Rocco's right leg, from where drops of blood oozed.

A versatile priest, Tobias, bandaged and attended to Rocco before taking him to the nearby health center, almost forty-five minutes away. The health center referred the critical case to the town hospital, another fifty kilometers (thirty miles) from the center.

"Where is the stone?" Father Tobias asked.

Father Tobias had placed a snakebite stone to remove the poison from the blood inside the bandage. The stone is supposed to fall away once the toxin is absorbed entirely in it.

"We threw it away. Now, you don't have to worry," the attending doctor assured. "The stone is fake."

Even after a dose of antivenom, seminarian Rocco showed signs of nausea and vomiting. He lost consciousness.

"It was the stone that kept him alive," Father Tobias said. "The two-hour delay would have killed him by now if not for the stone."

The stone, found in the dustbin, was secretly attached back on the wounds of Rocco. The medicinal rock did its job: it saved a life.

Due to delays in medical assistance, around fifty thousand people die because of snakebites every year in India.

70

Priest Fails to Stop Burial in a Backyard

Lucas, an African man, insisted that he be buried in the backyard of his home. The family members sent word to his son Kingsley, a newly ordained priest, to come and convince Lucas to be buried in the cemetery.

But Father Kingsley also failed to convince his father that the Catholic cemetery was a proper burial ground.

"Son, will I not go to heaven if I am buried at home?" Lucas had asked.

Father Kingsley asked the same question to his bishop, saying, "If you have an answer to this question, I will let my father know about it."

The matter was left unresolved due to the bishop's failure to provide an answer. Lucas searched for a reason to be buried away from his home.

Father Kingsley knew if his father was buried in the backyard, he would not be able to convince his mother to be buried in the cemetery.

"As a wife, she would want to be buried beside her husband," Father Kingsley told a friend.

A few months later, Lucas died. Father Kingsley buried his father behind their ancestral house in Africa. Father Kingsley's mother very much wants to be buried beside her husband, Lucas, after her death.

71

The Nuns Welcome a Con Priest

Victor, wearing a four-inch silver cross, knocked on a convent door. Sister Nora opened the door and thought the man to be a bishop.

"I am a priest," said Victor. Sister Nora ushered him into the parlor.

Forty-nine-year-old Victor stood like a stoic, holding a daily prayer book.

"I need a chapel to celebrate Mass," Victor said. "I am in town for a five-day seminar. I am staying in the hotel with lay participants of other faiths."

The nuns welcomed Victor as a priest with convent type hospitality, even a few sisters attended the Mass celebrated by Victor in the convent chapel.

"Father Victor, you are welcome to celebrate Mass tomorrow morning for our sisters," said Sister Ruby, the superior of the community.

"When a priest is available to celebrate Mass in the convent, the nuns avoided the trouble of walking half a mile to the church," Sister Ruby said.

Victor saw his opportunity. "Sure, what time?" Victor inquired.

After the morning Mass, Sister Ruby started a casual conversation, but Victor avoided giving details.

"Are you a diocesan or a religious order priest?" Sister Ruby asked.

"Diocesan," Victor replied. Victor talked about his expertise—retreats and seminars to priests, nuns, and families. Almost self-inviting himself, Victor said, "I can give a Bible session for your sisters."

Sister Ruby cross-checked with diocesan and religious priests about Victor.

Father Mason told Sister Ruby the story about Victor. Victor had entered the seminary in his forties but had dropped out within a year.

"Now Victor goes to convents to celebrate Mass or give retreats," Father Mason said.

Sister Ruby added, "Now, we have a con priest?"

About the Author

Feroz Fernandes, a Catholic missionary priest from Goa, India, shares dozens of incidents in a church setting. The author shares humorous and thought-provoking interactions among the church hierarchy, between priests and Catholics, and between priests and people of varied faith backgrounds. The author has a master of science degree in public service management from DePaul University, Chicago. Presently, the author is serving as a *Fidei donum* (Gift of Faith) priest in the Catholic Missions of Canada.